D1312630

For my own mom,

whose love and support

has taught me about helping others

and keeping promises. —J.S.

Published by Concordia Publishing House
3558 S. Jefferson Avenue, St. Louis, MO 63118-3968
1-800-325-3040 • www.cph.org

Text copyright © 2006 by Julie Stiegemeyer
Illustrations copyright © 2006 by Concordia Publishing House
Cover and interior fabric design © Coventry Cottage by Linda Hohag

All rights reserved. No part of this publication may be reproduced, stored in a retrieval system,
or transmitted, in any form or by any means, electronic, mechanical, photocopying, recording,
or otherwise, without the prior written permission of Concordia Publishing House.

Scripture quotations are from The Holy Bible, English Standard Version, copyright © 2001 by
Crossway Bibles, a division of Good News Publishers. Used by permission. All rights reserved.

Manufactured in China.

1   2   3   4   5   6   7   8   9   10   15   14   13   12   11   10   09   08   07   06

For weeks and months, you grew and grew

as we prepared for you to join our family.

When you arrived, we learned to care for you.
I marveled at your tiny fingers and toes. I watched
you sleep and memorized the curves of your face.

And I made promises I'm still learning to keep.

Foreword

I will gather you in my arms and wrap

you in warmth and love, just like

Mary held her infant Jesus.

For a time, God gave me your hands to hold, your tears to dry, your cheeks to kiss—God made you my child.

Even better, God adopts you as His own in Baptism. He forgives your sins. Now you are a child of God.

I will teach you to sing like angels about glad tidings for a Savior born among us, and I'll tell you about His redeeming death and an Easter resurrection. **I promise.**

I will give you the things you need:

 a warm coat for snowy days, a soft bed for

quiet nights, and your fuzzy blankey too.

I will scrub-a-dub you with bubbles

and let you play in the bath until

your fingertips are raisins.

I will hold your hand when we cross the street, and help you learn that obeying your parents keeps you safe. But I'll also let you learn to climb trees, although you might fall. I'll be ready with hugs and Band-Aids.

I will take time to listen—from your

first words to your curious questions.

And I'll do my best to answer why cats

have whiskers and where the wind

comes from.

I'll read you stories about foxes and crows, dogs and their bones. We'll read about quests and kings, children and a wardrobe. And I'll keep reading to you even after you read on your own.

We'll also read about how God split a sea in two, saved a man from lions, and made the blind see. In story after story, we'll learn about how God always keeps His promises. Every one.

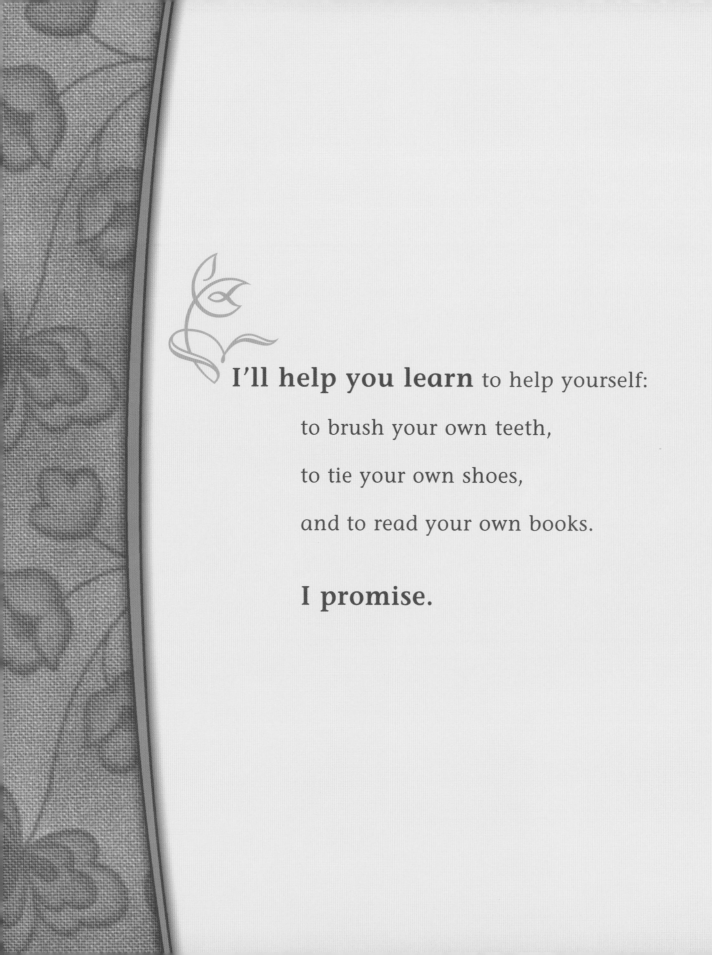

I'll help you learn to help yourself:

to brush your own teeth,

to tie your own shoes,

and to read your own books.

I promise.

I will give you all the foods that make you grow—chicken and carrots, cantaloupe and tomatoes from the farmers market. And we'll also make your favorite cookies often—peanut butter chocolate chip.

Together, we will give thanks for our food and all of God's gifts—even on tuna casserole night.

I will help you study your spelling words

and multiplication tables.

I'll also teach you that wisdom begins with

God's grace and knowing Jesus, our Savior.

I will reassure you that you are never alone—even when shadows lurk in the corners of your bedroom.

We will pray together and remember that God's angels guard us all through the night.

I promise.

 **I will cheer you on** from the sidelines, even when the game isn't going well. We'll talk about trying even when it's hard, being a friend to players who struggle, and showing grace in wins and losses.

Just like you, I'm still learning to listen

better, to pray even when I'm tired,

to be more patient. Only God is perfect,

so we'll ask for forgiveness together.

From your first steps to your first

home run, from your first day of school

to your graduation, and from your first

breath to your last, your heavenly Father

will care for you.

And I will love you all along the way.

I promise.